the fray how to save

© International Music Publications Ltd
International Music Publications Ltd is a Faber Music company
3 Queen Square, London WC1N 3AU

Printed in USA

ISBN10: 0-571-52948-8
EAN13: 978-0-571-52948-3

To buy Faber Music publications or to find out about the full range of titles available
please contact your local music retailer or Faber Music sales enquiries:

Faber Music Ltd, Burnt Mill, Elizabeth Way, Harlow CM20 2HX England
Tel: +44 (0) 1279 828982 Fax: +44 (0) 1279 828983
sales@fabermusic.com fabermusic.com

SHE IS

Words and Music by JOSEPH KING
and ISAAC SLADE

Do not get me wrong, I can-not wait for you to come
It's all up in the air and we stand still to see what comes

home. For now, you're not here and I'm not there.
down. I don't know where it is, I don't know when,

OVER MY HEAD
(Cable Car)

Words and Music by JOSEPH KING
and ISAAC SLADE

Moderately fast

I nev-er knew, I nev-er knew that ev-'ry-thing was
re-ar-range. I wish you were a stran-ger; I could

fall-ing through, that ev-'ry-one I knew was wait-ing on a cue to turn
dis-en-gage, just say ____ that we a-gree and then nev-er change, ____ soft-en ____

____ and run, ____ when all I need-ed was ____ the truth. ____ But that's ____ how it's got-
____ a bit un-til we all just get ____ a-long. _____ But that's dis-

my head, __ o- ver __ my head. With eight __ sec- onds __ left in o - ver- time, __ she's on __

your mind, __ she's on __ your __ mind. _____

Repeat and Fade

Optional Ending

HOW TO SAVE A LIFE

Words and Music by JOSEPH KING
and ISAAC SLADE

ALL AT ONCE

Words and Music by JOSEPH KING,
ISAAC SLADE and AARON JOHNSON

Moderately fast

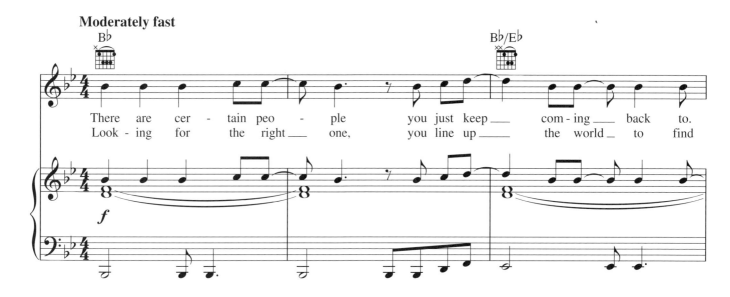

There are cer - tain peo - ple you just keep com - ing back to.
Look - ing for the right one, you line up the world to find

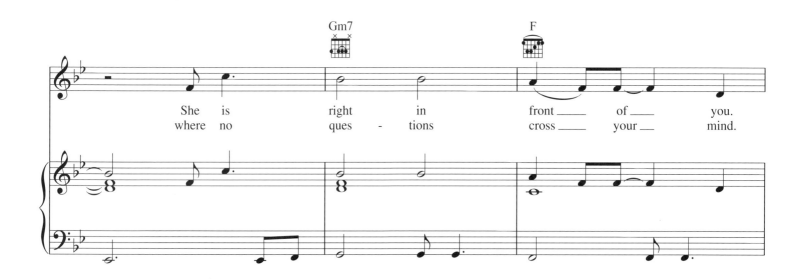

She is right in front of you.
where no ques - tions cross your mind.

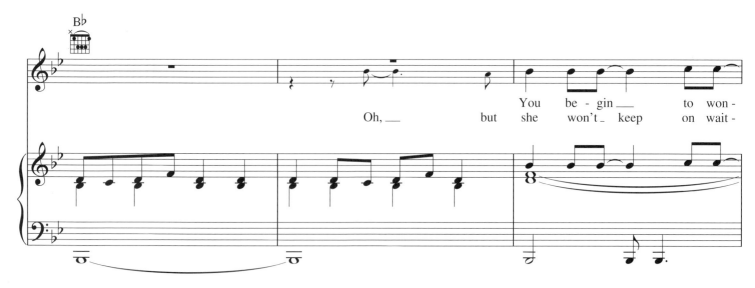

Oh, but she won't keep on wait - You be - gin to won -

FALL AWAY

Words and Music by JOSEPH KING
and ISAAC SLADE

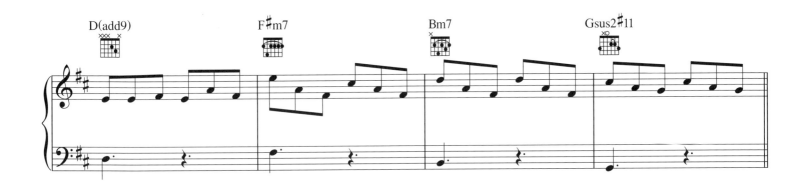

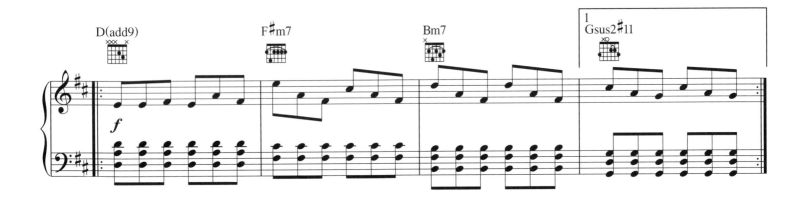

You swear you re - call
You left some - thing un - done,

HEAVEN FORBID

Words and Music by JOSEPH KING
and ISAAC SLADE

LOOK AFTER YOU

Words and Music by JOSEPH KING
and ISAAC SLADE

Slow Rock

If I don't say this now, __ I will sure-ly break __ as I'm leav-ing the one __ I want __ to take. __ For-give __ the ur-gen-cy, but hur-ry up __ and wait. __ My heart __ has start-ed to _____ sep - a - rate. _____ Oh, _____ oh, _____

D.S. al Coda

HUNDRED

Words and Music by ISAAC SLADE
and MONICA CONWAY

VIENNA

Words and Music by JOSEPH KING,
ISAAC SLADE and DANIEL BATTENHOUSE

The

day's   last ___ one - way ___   tick - et ___ train   pulls ___
ly   so ___ man - y ___   words that ___ we   can ___

DEAD WRONG

Words and Music by JOSEPH KING,
ISAAC SLADE and MICHAEL FLYNN

LITTLE HOUSE

Words and Music by JOSEPH KING
and ISAAC SLADE

Driving

She

does-n't look, _ she does-n't see, _ o-pens up _ for no - bod - y.

Fig - ures out, _____ she fig - ures out. _____

a - round.

Some-thing is scratch - ing its way ___ out, ___ some-thing you want ___ to for-get ___

mp

TRUST ME

Words and Music by JOSEPH KING
and ISAAC SLADE

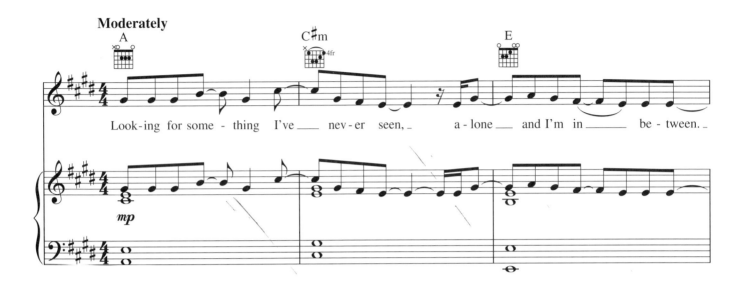

Look-ing for some - thing I've __ nev-er seen, __ a - lone __ and I'm in __ be - tween.

__ The place that I'm from __ and the place __ that I'm in, __ a

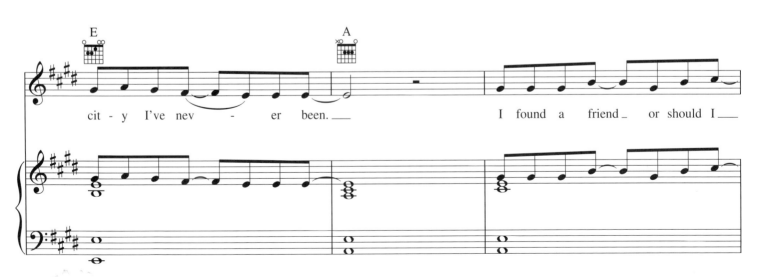

cit - y I've nev - er been. __ I found a friend __ or should I __